A POC on The Universal Automaton: An example of a Universal Automaton in ROBOTICS within Hospital Sector

Dr (Er) Om Prakash

Professor

Abstract

Pandemic like Covid-19 has once again highlighted the need to accelerate the companies, especially in healthcare to adopt automation. Countless doctors, nurses and health care workers have risked, are currently risking and may continue to risk their precious lives, while tending the dependents. Countless families have suffered as their lone bread winner succumbed to a risky act while tending Corona virus affected patients. The paper suggests that it is high time now that companies delegate the risky tasks to robots. The industry is currently in version 4.0, which is digitalization, and a universal need is felt to accelerate the companies towards adopting automation. Whilst automation is the next version in industrialization of the world, the question still arises as to whether state-of-art technologies are available to usher the companies towards the new era of automation or not. There are innumerable researches on Robotics and even the kids are being prepared to construct a robot at some places. However, seems to be aimless proliferation of robotics undertaking the ordinary or cliché jobs so much so that the whole activity appears clichéd. It is high time that a focused research is undertaken to construct a universal robot that can help to make robots that are secure, harmless to humans and replace preferably risky tasks. This will not only prepare the world in moving in right direction, but would also ensure safety and security of human race as the automation could be directed to replace only the risky tasks. This work is therefore aimed at constructing a universal "Automaton" to understand any requirement and assist in creating safe and secure robots with the help of 3D Printers. A prototype to this effect was developed and is available for further research and development in this area. A prototype and the paper has been submitted to ministries for approval. A Concept Paper was already submitted to this effect in the International Conference hosted by ICTCS in 2020.

Robots and artificial intelligence: An aid to dependent people ABSTRACT In the world of digitalization and automation, there were surprising myths co-existent that were not only surprising, but also ironic. Whilst the move is on to usher into the world of automation, where even the manufacturing units are devising the methods to automate their functions, it is only ironic to note that people have also developed several myths on using a robot. For one, robot has been associated with a device that would take away one job. For another, robot is considered risky as if it will start ruling the very person that made it. Apparently, research gap exists that needs to be plugged along with the understanding gaps to demystify the use of robots. Covid-19 has brought the

world to such a stage where companies are now rethinking about the use of robot. This paper is written to demystify the use on robots, clarify the need of robots in the society and present the growing demand of this technology. A research was also conducted to present the availability and state-of-art robot technology. It was also shown in the paper as to how some domains like healthcare is in dire need of robots, as the pandemic continues to wreak havoc on society.

Keywords: Robots, Artificial intelligence, dependent people, TIAGo

Introduction

We often see robots and artificial intelligence systems as intruders who can steal jobs from us or make decisions against humans. However, the truth is that these devices are already helping to improve people's lives. For example, these have been shown to be effective in support tasks for people with disabilities. These robots are already playing a vital role in the services to the elderly people who have developed some disabilities or the rehabilitation of patients with injuries. Robots are also being deployed for patients with the chronic pathologies. Besides, robots have been used in heavy industries where the working conditions are extreme like working near the furnaces.

This deployment has is already saving human lives. Robot is the most 'human' side of artificial intelligence.

Automation in medicine: transforming healthcare

- Contemporary medicine faces monumental challenges stemming from the increasing complexity of diseases, an aging population, and the need for more efficient and personalized medical care.

- In this scenario, automation emerges as a fundamental tool that directly responds to the growing demands and needs of the healthcare sector.

Today, the complexity of healthcare, driven by scientific and technological advances, demands a more agile and precise response. The workload on healthcare professionals is overwhelming, and this is where automation proves to be an indispensable ally.

This places the medical sector at a key moment to take advantage of a technological revolution, driven by digitalization, that appears to be redefining the way we approach healthcare. The need for greater efficiency, precision, and accessibility in healthcare services has led to a constant search for innovative solutions.

In this context, automation emerges as an essential catalyst for overcoming the challenges facing modern medicine. From data management to clinical decision-making, automation can offer concrete solutions to the current demands and limited resource capacity in the healthcare sector.

Advantages of automation in medicine

Automation in medicine is radically transforming healthcare, improving efficiency, precision, and personalization. As technology advances, these automated innovations will continue to play a crucial role in the constant evolution of healthcare, providing effective solutions to contemporary challenges in the field of medicine.

Among this list of benefits are:

1. Operational efficiency : Automation optimizes internal processes, reducing the time spent on administrative tasks and allowing healthcare professionals to focus on direct patient care.

According to recent studies, the implementation of automated systems in medical records management has been shown to reduce wait times and improve operational efficiency by 30%.

2. Diagnostic Accuracy : Automation in medical diagnosis, such as the use of machine learning algorithms, has significantly improved the accuracy of clinical assessments. This not only speeds up disease identification but also minimizes human error. Data reveals that the accuracy rate for AI-assisted diagnoses has exceeded 95% in various medical specialties.

3. Treatment Personalization : The ability to process large data sets enables the customization of treatment plans. Automation, by analyzing genomic, historical, and environmental data, facilitates the identification of personalized treatments, improving the effectiveness of therapies and reducing side effects.

4. Improving ongoing care : Automated patient monitoring systems have transformed ongoing care. From wearable devices to remote monitoring systems, automation facilitates constant monitoring, alerting healthcare professionals to

significant changes in a patient's health, enabling early interventions, and preventing complications.

Major innovations for the medical sector

At the forefront of the healthcare revolution, innovations in automation are paving the way for new possibilities. From surgical precision to the acceleration of medical research, these innovations are redrawing the boundaries of what's possible in modern medicine.

Among the cutting-edge and promising innovations that are taking automation to the next level, catapulting healthcare toward a more efficient, precise, and patient-centric future, the following stand out:

1. Advanced surgical robotics : Automation has led to the evolution of surgical robotics , enabling more precise and less invasive procedures. Systems like the Da Vinci Surgical System have already proven effective in complex surgeries, offering faster recovery and fewer postoperative complications.

2. Artificial Intelligence in Medical Research : Artificial intelligence (AI) has become an essential

tool in medical research. From discovering new drugs to identifying patterns in large clinical data sets, automation through AI is accelerating the pace of medical innovation.

3. Automation-Powered Telemedicine : Automation boosts telemedicine by enabling efficient transmission of medical data, virtual consultations, and remote follow-up. This not only improves accessibility to medical care, especially in remote areas, but also optimizes long-term health management.'

Robots conquer the health field

There's a lot of talk about automation and robotics applied to Industry 4.0. Sectors such as the automotive, aeronautical and aerospace, and food industries have greatly benefited from them. However, the development of robots in the healthcare field has been of great importance due to the value they bring in situations where precision is vital.

We're used to talking about the advantages that robotics offers in industry . At the production level, automation, combined with digitalization, has been a major revolution.

The introduction of connectivity and technology in factories has boosted other jobs that can enhance innovation, especially avoiding those related to repetitive tasks that don't add value to the activity, or those involving dangerous actions or the handling of substances that could put workers at risk. Furthermore, this way, companies can implement more efficient and flexible production, as production adapts to market needs.

Regarding the use of robotics in the healthcare sector, this technology has changed the way patients and their health are treated in many ways. The fields of research, surgery, medication management and organization, and even rehabilitation have greatly benefited from the development of this innovative field.

The precision

Robotics applied to manufacturing allows human talent to be leveraged in tasks that add value to companies. It also reduces people's exposure to dangerous situations and minimizes potential errors caused by the "human factor." In addition to all these advantages, the precision this technology can offer when applied to the healthcare sector is particularly noteworthy.

In reality, robots can perform gestures that mimic those a doctor would perform, but their precision is much greater. This doesn't mean they will replace medical personnel, nor that human care will disappear. It's about taking advantage of all the benefits that technological innovation brings and using these tools, which facilitate the work of specialists.

Robotic gynecology

Following the line of precision, developments in various fields of medicine continue to grow. One example is the use of robots in gynecology. It may seem like a science fiction story, but it has long been a reality. Years ago, the Polish University of Science and Technology, together with the Danish company Universal Robots, launched a project to introduce stem cells into patients' bodies through surgical procedures capable of offering greater precision than that of the human hand.

Another project carried out by both organizations was the creation of a mixing station for cytotoxic drugs used in cancer chemotherapy. This attempt was to solve the problem of working with certain potentially toxic elements and doing so for longer periods of time, as these tasks were limited to a few hours of work by the scientific staff.

Sensitive robots in the hospital

In the face of a health crisis, caring for a patient without fear of infection at the height of the transmission peak, and simultaneously protecting the health of healthcare workers and patients, are priority actions. This is possible thanks to a project carried out by a group of researchers from Simon Fraser University in Canada, who have developed robots capable of performing medical assistant tasks such as measuring temperature, heart rate, and respiratory rate.

This device consists of two robots, one humanoid in shape and the other with a robotic arm equipped with sensors capable of receiving, through biomedical electrodes, a significant amount of information about the patient, reducing interactions with medical personnel and minimizing the risk of infection when performing basic tasks. Both tools could be used for primary care, including more complicated surgeries, in geographical areas where healthcare is unavailable.

Combination with other technologies

The application of Artificial Intelligence has also been decisive in promoting this area of study. Software development for healthcare robots facilitates patient monitoring and telemedicine. In this regard, the Automation, Robotics, and Mechatronics Group at the University of Almería , together with the American company InTouch Health, is working on the design of a mobile robot that performs basic examinations and can navigate around the medical center. According to the digital magazine novaciencia.es, these tools, which are already present in hospitals in the United States and Germany, are equipped with a GPS sensor and software that provides them with perception.

Robots for the heart

Interventional cardiology procedures have also changed. Thanks to the Siemens Corindus robotic system, a pioneer in Southern Europe and of which there are only 15 in the entire region, the system aims to increase the precision and safety of coronary interventions, reduce radiation exposure to both patients and healthcare personnel, and shorten procedure times.

This system uses ultra-high-resolution imaging to enable precise monitoring of catheters and guidewires, as well as balloon and stent implants. Since June 2021, Corindus has been used at the Gregorio Marañón Hospital in Madrid, in surgeries for patients suffering from angina or myocardial infarction, benefiting 65 patients.

Dependent people

They are those who have developed a health conditions or exist with a condition that makes them in the need of others help. For example, old people or people with special needs or people who have developed a health condition, which makes them dependent on help and support of care takers. One special example on today's context are people who have contracted the pandemic disease of Covid-19. The diseases is such infectious that if someone contacts this disease, the person is immediately quarantined in a hospital. In such case, the subject is completely dependent on all day-to-day need on the caretakers. In effect, the caretaker is able to provide only limited support as the caretakers are also at grave risk of contracting such disease. This means that the scenario is already set to take the technology in health care domain to the next level, where a device like robot may give such a risky care. Today, as the statistics reveal, almost 20 per cent of the worldwide population may be living in a stage where they might heavily depend on others. Such dependency has to be taken-up by a robot, and once again the society needs a dire and immediate help from technology.

Robots and AI immediately needed

Robots are the devices, which automate some human action with the help of some intelligence built-in for their operations. This intelligence simulates human intelligence, at least to some level. Such intelligence, which has been artificially built by developers, is termed as artificial intelligence. Robots, powered by such artificial intelligence can help people who are severely dependent on others. Imagine old person, who is left with no one to help and lives in a condition that makes him almost impossible to get-up from the bed to fulfill some daily needs. Arguably, there is no solution better than placing a robot to help such a person who cannot even get-up to fill water for himself. In other case, many people who have contracted Covid-19 disease and are quarantined and caretakers are very cautious in dealing with them. Pandemic has almost certainly proved the immediate need of large number of robots to be acquired by any health care center.

TIAGo Robot helping people with condition

It is now not unknown that countless people with a medical condition are employing robots to help them. Earlier there were joint families where old people or people with some condition or disability were helped by their relatives. Nowadays, old people or people who have developed a condition have no option but to live all alone. This is so as the trend nowadays is to live in nuclear families or even as single parent or elementary families. Frequently, few people find themselves living all alone. In that case, they either employ a nurse or a helper, but, as their physical condition is challenge, it leaves them to the complete mercy of such helpers. There have been security issues reported (Pages, Marchionni & Ferro, 2016). Fortunately, in the age of digitalization and automation, as the industries are preparing to enter into industry 5.0 – automation, there are devices like TIAGoRobot, to help those who have a medical condition or certain disability.

TIAGois now available to lend a hand in whatever it takes. The device has one arm and no feet but a round base that turns and rolls on the ground. It has a face, somewhat similar to what one saw in the sci-fi movies Wall.E's and ET's, where a smile is always drawn. TIAGorobot is an acronym that means 'Take It And Go!' and is able to help with household chores to an elderly person, or a severe disability, who lives alone at home.And not only that -- through its optical sensor, this robot can know how that person is and communicate with them to ask what they need at all times. A nurse can monitor the person from a distance to provide simple care for that person and thus avoid having to travel to the health center. Sometimes, it is only necessary for someone to be aware that no accident happens to the subject when that person goes to a place like bathroom. Some patients would not mind even if a device accompanies them to certain places, whereas they would have discomfort if a person like nurse accompanies then to washroom, especially if they have severe disabilities. This is how the TIAGo robot can be programmed to help and is even capable of placing a blanket well on the bed at night if the subject happens to be uncovered (Mocanu, et. al. 2018). TIAGo is very much there in the market and it is a great news for many. The models are manufactured by PAL Robotics, a leading company in robotics applied to assistance to people with various medical conditions. Robot can support to subjects suffering from sight, hearing impairment or disability in ambulation as well as other medical conditions like Alzheimer's disease. The latter psychological conditions develops in many old people, who appear to be normal but actually are severely limited. They need someone to keep reminding them of simple things as they get increasingly forgetful. Judith Viladomat, Head of Communication, explains that the company's mission is precisely that robots can improve people's lives in different aspects. "One of them is helping elderly or disabled people with household chores. If a robot can do these tasks, the lives of these people improve." (Lafrenz, 2017).

Goal of Robotics to help growing population of elderly people in the society

Statistics indicated that the elderly population is growing gradually. Health care has improved a lot, as there is cure for several diseases that were incurable a few decades ago. There is cure for cancer and other deadly diseases, which is responsible for increasing the average life expectancy. Life expectancy is increasing as a result of healthcare improvement, which indicates that the elderly population will grow a lot in the coming decades.

However, it will be increasingly difficult to reach all the people who need some human means or intervention. Companies like PAL Robotics are now increasingly aware of this horizon. "There are many studies that say that there will not be enough resources in long-term care to provide assistance to everyone in a dignified and quality way. That is why robotics is entering this field," says Viladomat(Lafrenz, 2017). The Robotics companies also do not believe that robots will conflict with caregivers, as there are a lot of things that a human being contributes that a robot cannot supply. Their goal is not to make robot friends that have intelligence and simulate the emotions or feelings, just like a human being. There object is to make tools with the ability to interact with the environment and help people who have limiting conditions using advanced concepts of Artificial Intelligence (AI) and machine learning (ML). With this development, robots are going to fill jobs that may involve physical risk for nurses or caregivers (Grama&Rusu, 2019). As we are in the age of Covid-19, one can imagine the potential of robots. They can save countless lives of caregivers, as for sure the Covid-19 virus cannot affect a robot. These can interact in close vicinity with the patient without risking the lives of countless caregivers. Incidentally, the statistics reports that many precious lives of health care workers like those of nurses were lost or affected by Covid-19 as their job was just to work closely with patients. They had to help the patients with severe infection like providing them life support or helping them in their chores. On the other hand, a robot can be trained or programmed to work closely with a patient like providing them ordinary things like medicine dosages, water, or any other similar activity. Robots also help in lifting a lot of weight like reclining beds and they will always be controlled by one person. In addition, robots can have a wide spectrum of vision and detect things that a person is not able to see(Lafrenz, 2017).. Robotics Development

Several Robotics companies now predict that in a matter of five years they will see "TIAGos" in private homes. In a longer period of time humanoids will also enter the scene. Humanoids are also termed sometimes as bipedal robots, with an anatomy and stature similar to those of the human beings. With the help of AI/ML based programming, these devices will be able to adapt one hundred percent to the external environment where they would work. These would be designed according to human anatomy and biology. Currently the development of humanoids is being slower than that of other models due to navigation and displacement problems.

Hand-made

The main burden for integrating robots into people's daily lives is their high price. Many Robotics models are handcrafted in-house and very few units are made commercially. This brings the price of the most basic TIAGo model to 30,000 euros and the most complete ones to 60,000 Euros. In the case of humanoids, the cost may be between 150,000 to 900,000 Euros. Currently, there is still no demand for this kind of technology, but once people try it and see that it is useful, they will be marketed to end users, and not just to university R&D departments, etc. Robotics companies as of now are completely convinced, as it happened with the automobiles or the computers, that when the demand increases and they are mass manufactured for commercial purposes, they would come at an affordable price. A robot will cost the same as a car. However, for this, it is necessary that fears and prejudices towards robots that come from the plots of science fiction novels and films, must disappear. Growing fear as developed by some science fiction or myths about robotsderives an apprehension when a subject meets his or her robot for the first time. Thus, as the subject meets for the first time the robotic assistant, it is inevitable that this strangeness appears mixed with a certain fear. At first, some older people don't like it. However, it happens only in the first moment: when they see what it can and cannot do, the limits it has and how they can control it, these fears disappear. Robots are machines, they are programmed by people and depend on them, and just like other machines like cars or fans or any other devices to make our lives easier, robots help people and there is no reason to fear them.

Rehabilitation robots

At the National Hospital for Paraplegics in Toledo, there are two robots that carry out their work every day normally. These are the Locomat, which adhere to the legs of the spinal cord injured to help them in their rehabilitation march. "They have been involved in the rehabilitation of people for 10 years now. It is one more treatment, as is physiotherapy, occupational therapy, etc," explains Antonio del Ama, head of the Biomechanics and Technical Aids Unit at the hospital(del-Ama, et.al., 2014). In addition, in the center there are three units of another type of ambulatory robot for gait compensation (del-Ama, et.al., 2014). "We are investigating its effectiveness in the rehabilitation of patients. They were built with the idea that the patient would take them home and do their daily life with them, but they are also attracting a lot of attention as rehabilitators,"says Del Ama (Torricelli et.al., 2015).

Exoskeletons help in the rehabilitation of spinal cord injuries

Before the appearance of the Locomat, the intensive repetition of the gait movement, which the patient must do as a fundamental therapy for his or her rehabilitation, was an immense effort for physiotherapists. The patients were placed on a treadmill, supported from above with a harness. Two physiotherapists moved his legs manually while another held his body. After 10-15 minutes, the physiotherapists were physically exhausted (del-Ama, et.al., 2014). Now thanks to these robots, the movement can be repeated for hours. The limit is not the fatigue of the physiotherapists but the fatigue of the patient.There is false fear that their jobs will be taken away, but it is a paradigm shift (Torricelli et.al., 2015). This leads the person in charge of the Biomechanics Unit to make the following reflection: "AI and robotics are usually seen as a threat. There are those who fear that jobs will be taken away from us, but in my opinion, what occurs is a paradigm shift. It does not make sense that there are three physiotherapists moving the legs of a patient when there is a robot that can do it and those three professionals may be treating other patients" (Frizera, et.al, 2012).Del Ama affirms that there are more and more people with disabilities, and we must give the best possible service to all. "In this area, to the extent that robots and machines can help us to carry out automated processes, we will be able to serve more patients with the same staff, and also have better control over therapy," he says (Torricelli et.al., 2015). The drawback of these systems, according to Del Ama, is their "excessively expensive" price (del-Ama, et.al., 2014). Something that the head of the Biomechanics Unit attributes to the fact that the application of robotics in this area is still in a very incipient phase: "It is something that is being born now. In order to implement one of these treatments, it is necessary to show from the scientific point of view that it is really positive for the patient and to know well all its effects " (Torricelli et.al., 2015). While the research phase lasts, the demand for these devices will be irrelevant and, consequently, the prices will continue to be exorbitant. But in the long term, everything indicates that robots will end up being regular human cooperators in a multitude of tasks and a very useful tool to respond to the needs of dependent people(Frizera, et.al, 2012).

AI as neurological therapy

Josep Lluís Arcos, from the Artificial Intelligence Research Institute (CSIC) is in charge of three of the most advanced machine learning projects applied to cognitive stimulation and rehabilitation. The Innobrain and Cognitio projects benefit people with degenerative diseases, while Amate helps people with autism spectrum disorders (ASD) to show their emotions (Arcos, De Mantaras& Serra, 1998).Arcos assures that a large number of AI and machine learning projects are emerging in the area of neurology that, although they are in an incipient phase, are already beginning to show great potential. "There are projects that, by exploiting GPS technology, allow people with neurodegenerative diseases to be given more autonomy by monitoring their movements and helping in the event of disorientation or loss," explains the researcher (Plaza, Arcos, & Martin, 1996). On the other hand, the Amate project arises from the need to develop technologies that help families and therapists in the day-to-day life of children with ASD and to solve one of the problems they present is the difficulty to identify their emotions as for example the stress that an unexpected situation can cause you (Sierra et.al., 204). "We are using wristbands with biometric sensors such as movement and changes in conductivity of the skin," says the IIIA researcher, who continues: "Our system incorporates machine learning algorithms that allow us to customize the identification of behaviors, and their meaning, to each child. In other words, after a few hours of initial training, the system is capable of adapting to the needs of each child." (Arcos & de Mántaras, 1997).

Robots for Covid-19 and other Pandemics

As in science fiction, the coronavirus pandemic has made the interaction between humans and robots natural today and even more so when the best barrier to contagion is to avoid social contact. "The pandemic opens the eyes of organizations to realize that robots are required to avoid one-on-one contact," said Aldo Luévano, CEO of Roomie, the Mexican engineering firm that developed the robot.Luévano explained that with the support of large technology companies they seek to demonstrate that the development of this type of technology and the implementation of robotics is possible in Mexico and that is why they developed, in just two weeks, a robot capable of helping in the diagnosis of coronavirus (Mario, 2020). The company worked with two infectologists and relied on technology from Intel, which provides artificial intelligence and processing solutions to analyze large amounts of data, and from Amazon Web Services, which provides the cloud, machine learning and the analysis and identification of people and places through Amazon Rekognition(Mario, 2020). Luévano explained that the company has been in Mexico for six years developing humanoid robots for assistance in sectors such as tourism, retail and banks and that the pandemic gave them the opportunity to create a robot to help public and private medical institutions to serve possible cases of patients with coronavirus. "The robot is programmed to perform hospital triage," he said. However, he said he does not seek and cannot make a diagnosis, he only guides people to know if they are suspected of suffering from coronavirus(Mario, 2020).

Discussion

Need of robots have been increasingly felt, not only by companies, but also society. As the robots have gradually entered the market, companies, homes and even commercial places, the myths related to robots are being shattered. The myths that the robots are going to take jobs, or that robots would be security threats are now being rejected as a myth. Many science fiction movies are responsible to establish the myths and some of them are so weird that they claim that ultimately robots may rule society. The state-of-art of development of robot is still in the nascent stage. There are only specific areas where robots are proving helpful like providing a helping hand to people who are dependent on others for their daily chores. Covid-19 has sealed the issue in favor of robots. Many caretakers have contracted the deadly disease while treating Covid patients. Caretakers like nurses have to give all-round service for extended hours. Some nurses contracted the disease and risked their lives especially as a robot can easily carry such activities. For example, a robot can be present at the hospital and provide services like taking temperature, providing medicine doses, providing helping hand to patients in their miscellaneous need during their quarantine states, and most importantly relieve nurses with some of their utmost busiest schedules. Arguably, robots are the best way to serve people who are living with some physical or mental condition that makes them constantly dependent on others. This is especially true if a person also has no alternative but to live alone and in that case, it is also being regarded as best for the safety and security of the person living alone. Robot is programmed to do just the specific activity and will not have enough "brains" to plot some mischief. Moreover, the company who supplies robot can also remotely monitor the robot functioning and would work ethically and in a responsible manner. A pandemic to develop robots The Roomiebot Covid-19 is equipped with technologies to detect possible cases of coronavirus and that is why it was developed in conjunction with two infectologists.Luévano explained that this tool comes equipped with a thermometer and an oximeter that allows the detection of dyspnea, or shortness of breath, a common condition among patients with the disease.The idea, he said, is not to replace medical personnel, but to streamline the process of caring for potential patients. With this tool, he explained, what is sought is to avoid the collapse of medical institutions due to lack of personnel by letting the first line of contact be a robot that, in case of detecting symptoms in a patient, can channel it effectively. The robot is capable of identifying symptoms such as cough, headache, arthralgia, myalgia, odynophagia, rhinorrhea, conjunctivitis and chest pain and can also obtain demographic or clinical data to identify patients at increased risk for pre-existing diseases. Roomie Robot will reach hospitals The need to avoid contact between people is required so as not to generate more infections. These types of models also help in the disinfection of spaces such as hospitals or workplaces, in the delivery of packages or in the support of information without human contact, minimizing the risk. "From issues of delivery (distribution) of medicines and meals, to issues of robots that can count responses, you need to have use cases and contactless technology (payment without cash)," he said.Now, the media has also been pro-active to highlight the keys that stop Covid-19 in the countries. One key measure to stop the further spread is the use of robots.

Conclusion

The health care experts have not stressed that at this time somemedical firms do have the capacity to deploy hundreds of robots that can be used in hospitals, companies and airports, and it is expected that in about few weeks they will have a presence in at least some hospitals and other facilities. The experts also explained that in the case of robots like TIAGo Robot and Roomiebot Covid-19, the firms are willing to operate in the joint venture model, in which the medical institutions cover some expenses for the robot's raw material to allow its use and impact to expand rapidly. They have noted that while the investment cost is high, this will never be compared to the value of a human life.Robots came not to replace humans but, in this type of pandemic, but they give value to people.

References

Arcos, J. L., De Mantaras, R. L., & Serra, X. (1998). Saxex: A case-based reasoning system for generating expressive musical performances. Journal of New Music Research, 27(3), 194-210. Arcos, J. L., & de Mántaras, R. L. (1997, July). Perspectives: a declarative bias mechanism for case retrieval. In International Conference on Case-Based Reasoning (pp. 279-290). Springer, Berlin, Heidelberg. (Mario, 2020). Mexican robot is a useful tool in the battle against the coronavirus. Burgeron Report. Retrieved from https://burgeronreport.com/mexican-robot-is-a-useful-tool-in-the-battle-against-the-coronavirus-video/ del-Ama, A. J., Gil-Agudo, Á., Pons, J. L., & Moreno, J. C. (2014). Hybrid gait training with an overground robot for people with incomplete spinal cord injury: a pilot study. Frontiers in human neuroscience, 8, 298. Frizera, A., Elias, A., Del-Ama, A. J., Ceres, R., & Bastos, T. F. (2012, June). Characterization of spatio-temporal parameters of human gait assisted by a robotic walker. In 2012 4th IEEE RAS & EMBS International Conference on Biomedical Robotics and Biomechatronics (BioRob) (pp. 1087-1091). IEEE. Grama, L., &Rusu, C. (2019, October). Extending Assisted Audio Capabilities of TIAGo Service Robot. In 2019 International Conference on Speech Technology and Human-Computer Dialogue (SpeD) (pp. 1-8). IEEE. Lafrenz, R. Archive 2017. Mocanu, I., Axinte, D., Cramariuc, O., &Cramariuc, B. (2018, July). Human Activity Recognition with Convolution Neural Network Using TIAGo Robot. In 2018 41st International Conference on Telecommunications and Signal Processing (TSP) (pp. 1-4). IEEE. Pages, J., Marchionni, L., & Ferro, F. (2016,

October). Tiago: the modular robot that adapts to different research needs. In International workshop on robot modularity, IROS. Plaza, E., Arcos, J. L., & Martin, F. (1996). Cooperative case-based reasoning. In Distributed Artificial Intelligence Meets Machine Learning Learning in Multi-Agent Environments (pp. 180-201). Springer, Berlin, Heidelberg. Sierra, C., Rodriguez-Aguilar, J. A., Noriega, P., Esteva, M., & Arcos, J. L. (2004). Engineering multi-agent systems as electronic institutions. European Journal for the Informatics Professional, 4(4), 33-39. Torricelli, D., Del Ama, A. J., Gonzalez, J., Moreno, J., Gil, A., & Pons, J. L. (2015, July). Benchmarking lower limb wearable robots: Emerging approaches and technologies. In Proceedings of the 8th ACM International Conference on PErvasive Technologies Related to Assistive Environments (pp. 1-4).